**Made in America
to be shared with the world**

www.pausebreatheproceed.com

©2022 Pause Breathe Proceed LLC. All rights reserved. No part of this book may be reproduced in any form without written permission from the author. This book is designed to provide information and insight. Please understand that the authors and publisher are not rendering any type of psychological, legal, or any other kind of professional advice. Neither the publisher nor the author(s) shall be liable for any physical, psychological, emotional, financial, or commercial damages, including, but not limited to, special, incidental, consequential or other damages. You are responsible for your own choices, actions, and results. Never disregard professional medical advice or delay seeking it.

Library of Congress Control Number: 2023903950

Pause, Breathe, Proceed, LLC., written by Karen Wright. **Boyne City, Michigan 49712 USA**

From our readers

Thank you so much Karen! The day I read this I was struggling with something heavy and I decided to try your advice, *"When I pause I simply ask WHAT am I feeling, thinking, about to say or do? Really check into your body and mind. Then belly breathe. This will tell the Vagus nerve to tell the brain to calm the body and mind. Ask yourself WHY? Keep asking WHY until you get to the real cause."* Wow! I couldn't believe it! It was so helpful. It got me unstuck and unwound my big feelings. I am very appreciative of such a simple and effective tool. It worked!! I use it when I get stuck. I appreciate your efforts in helping me find greater peace.

    – Tammy Light, California

Engaging in Pause Breathe Proceed has improved my awareness of how I engage with people and events, and to understand how my past shapes my response. It has helped me to pause, breathe and think about my response rather than simply reacting to a person or situation. It also gave me strategies to be "OK" with stepping away from a situation to think about my feelings and a better, more compassionate response. In this world of difficult politics, COVID, crime and war, it is easy to become overwhelmed with anger and frustration. PBP is a great strategy for coping at this time in our world. I would recommend PBP to everyone, including children.

    – Nancy Epstein, Michigan

Too often we are our own worst enemy. Self criticism and condemnation become the norm. This book shows us the way to become our own best friend again. The concepts are simple and easy to learn and the results can be life changing.

– *Jenelle Cummings, Minnesota*

When I first heard about Pause Breathe Proceed, I thought it was going to be a tad on the "misty" side, with pictures of beautiful people finding inner peace sitting in the lotus position on a rock overlooking a beach. I could not have been more mistaken! Pause Breathe Proceed is a common sense power tool that anyone can use, anywhere. Karen Wright has taken complicated theories of mindfulness and emotional intelligence and boiled them down into the simplest of simple techniques that we can bring straight into our everyday lives, no yoga mat required!

– *Kecia Freed, Michigan*

But also great opportunity!

POWER

"Until you make the unconscious conscious,
it will direct your life and you will call it fate."
— Carl Jung

The power of Pause Breathe Proceed

Pause Breathe Proceed reduces stress, improves health and empowers free will

Pause Breathe Proceed directs you to a life of peace, understanding, healthy relationships, compassion, and joy. Pause Breathe Proceed empowers personal changes that lead to improved physical, mental, emotional, and social health as well as improving relationships with oneself and others. It is mindfulness and emotional intelligence in action.

To pause and breathe is an ancient game changer. It is the STOP button of life to remind you to slow down, regroup, and take action toward improved life focus and health. Without pausing throughout your day, throughout your life, you move forward like a freight train. You forget where you're going and why. You can miss the wonderful stops along the way. At the end of your life, you will look back and wonder what happened to those dreams and moments in life that make living worthwhile.

It took me two years to come up with my elevator speech: *"Pause Breathe Proceed is the tool that allows you to calmly and consciously make choices that break subconscious thought patterns and allow you to live the life you choose."*

I struggled with health issues my whole life due to stress. As a massage therapist of twenty years, I wanted to understand stress and how it affects the body and mind. The practices of mindfulness and emotional intelligence came to my attention. I attended a week-long intensive retreat on the neuroscience of yoga and meditation. At the retreat, I lived mindfully or in the present moment. I was aware of what I was doing and my surroundings were peaceful. Stress was reduced. Well, of course it was! I had meals prepared for me, attended classes, and performed mindful exercises.

When I got back to my daily life, being mindful and in the moment was impossible. I was like a squirrel. My attention span was all over the place. I needed to understand why mindfulness was so hard.

I looked to the sky, asked God for guidance, and three powerful words came to me, "Pause Breathe Proceed."

These three words are a reminder to stop that freight train the mind and body live on. Our brain is wired to react in a certain way to just about every situation. This wiring tells us impulsively what to think, say, and do.

Pause Breathe Proceed is a simple process anyone can incorporate throughout the day to rewire the brain. Catching your reaction and being aware simply requires a pause and a deep breath to check in with yourself and the situation around you. What is going on? What thoughts, feelings, and emotions are happening and what behaviors are they creating?

Mindfulness (being fully present) + emotional intelligence (control of your emotions) = emergency brakes on your reactive brain train. You have opportunity to pivot and become your own neuroscientist, to rewire your brain to respond differently and find peace.

Emotional intelligence? It took me a while to put that piece into the puzzle. My generation grew up playing outside until dark and even after dark. We had encyclopedias instead of Google, and our brains were seldom overloaded since reading an encyclopedia wasn't going to happen.

We cried, laughed, played, fought, and hung out. Our emotions processed through us on a daily basis.

Now we are so disconnected from our body, mind and each other that we don't identify with our emotions. The bad ones we call "stress" and keep moving on. Without identifying them, without being emotionally intelligent, we just bury them and wonder why our stress increases. Buried emotions cause physical and mental issues.

Emotional intelligence is the awareness, understanding, and control of our emotions and managing them in a positive manner.

My husband, Kevin, is an engineer. He would never go to a yoga, meditation, or mindfulness class, but he can easily incorporate Pause Breathe Proceed into his day. He also reminds me to pause and breathe occasionally.

Although my life is not stress free, my stress is controlled and I am free. My physical, mental, emotional, and social health are strong. I am learning so much about myself. This is what I wish for you.

Please use the tools in this toolkit to start your journey to become calmer, kinder, open-hearted, and open-minded. Another great way to remember to pause breathe and proceed is to create a community of co-workers, friends, or family members who help one another to recognize reactive states and remind one another to pause and breathe before they proceed and to share stories of successes.

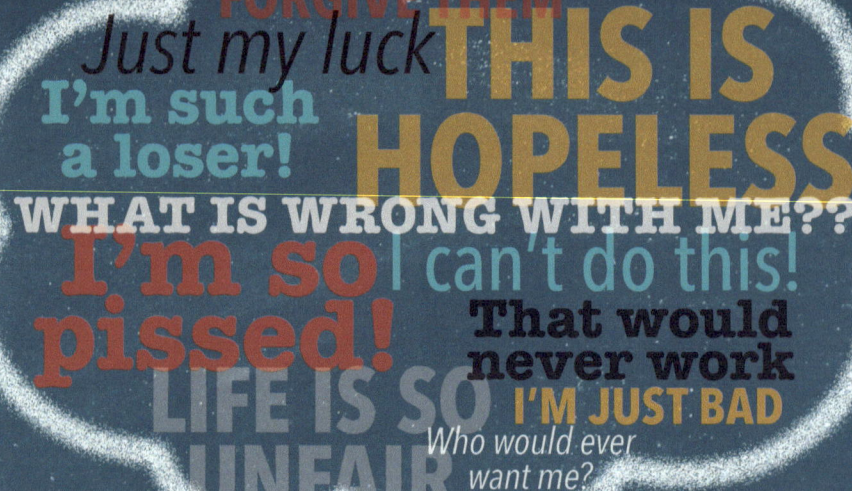

"A great many people think they are thinking when they are merely rearranging their prejudices."

– William James

Your thoughts

**Embracing a thought gives it power over
your life, choose thoughts wisely**

Thoughts and definitions throughout this toolkit are a combination of dictionary definitions, how an authority has explained a topic, how I heard what was explained, and how I experienced the word or topic. All definitions in life are subject to the author's knowledge and experiences.

The thoughts that result in acts of kindness and love are inherently ones to believe in. Those that result in fear, anger, or hate should be avoided. Know what thoughts live inside of you and feed the pause-itive ones so they become beliefs.

Authors are influenced by what they believe to be true. That is an important point to remember in life as you read social media, watch the news, or listen to others around you. Thoughts are opinions. Some are backed by fact. Some are backed by science. Some resonate with you, and most require you to explore deeper into their meaning.

In this age of technology there is information and disinformation. Learn to dig in and research the true meaning of important thoughts in your life. This keeps you true to yourself. That is what happened when I set out to understand mindfulness and emotional intelligence. I felt like a guppy in a sea of information.

This book is the accumulation of my thoughts. I hope it resonates with you. I have spent years creating this simple powerful way to incorporate mindfulness and emotional intelligence into daily living. I found peace by using Pause Breathe Proceed to understand my thoughts and who I am. This is what I wish for you.

What and who do you spend the most time with and why? How are you influenced by their thoughts? Pause and check into how the thoughts feel. Listen to thoughts and decide if you are going to believe that particular thought or not. Do some digging. Thoughts you believe in will shape your life. This may take a split second or weeks. As you learn who you are, you will come to know what you believe in.

"Passion is energy. Feel the power that comes from focusing on what excites you."

– Oprah Winfrey

Pause Breathe Proceed

**Opening hearts, freeing minds
with a pause and a breath**

Throughout life I have made choices to pivot. These choices came from an innate knowing that something needed to change. The more you take quiet time with yourself, the more you will know what feels right. Honing in on your values, goals, dreams, passions and purpose in life will give you razor focus, grit, heart, fortitude, strength, and determination to pivot. Working hard to enable each pivot gives you the pride and courage to do it on your own without the approval of anyone else.

In order to embrace Pause Breathe Proceed, it is important to understand its value. It improves health by reducing stress, but what is stress? Our thoughts create our stress, so where do thoughts come from and why? It also improves relationships, but how? These are questions I had to answer to understand why Pause Breathe Proceed, or mindfulness + emotional intelligence, work.

Thoughts are ideas we accumulate during our lifetime. Thoughts are fed to us by our parents and how they raised us, our teachers and what they taught us, our friends and the generation we grow up in, the media and their agenda. The list goes on. As you can see, we all grew up with different ideas of the world, our life, and our purpose.

Understanding that everyone's thoughts come from different places allows understanding and compassion instead of judgment. With Pause Breathe Proceed it is possible to know your thoughts, own your reactions, and realize that although raised differently, we can all learn from one other. We can come to an understanding, or agree to disagree. In the end, we can live in peace.

Following are the topics that I feel are important to understand the hows and whys of Pause Breathe Proceed. It can be as simple as pausing when your feathers get ruffled or at various times throughout the day. Pause Breathe Proceed can have beneficial application for a lifespan or a moment in time. There are times in life when a pause or time out for reflection is needed, and there are times in a day when a pause and a breath is required before proceeding.

If you do these three things throughout your day and make it a habit, you will start changing from the inside out.

Use your reminders. Wear your bracelet and place your stickers where you most likely will need a pause. Place them on a steering wheel or car dashboard to prevent road rage. Place them on a cell phone, computer, around work and at home to prevent a negative reaction.

Throw on your bracelet. Grab your credo card. Place your stickers strategically so you will remember to pause and breathe before you proceed and let's GO! What triggers you and when? Place a sticker smack dab in the middle of your trigger areas.

"Stress is an engineering term used to define the breaking point of a material."

– Joyce Meyers

Stress

Stress is simply a reflection of your thoughts both internal and external

Stress is how we interpret the craziness in our life. Our thoughts create our stress, our thoughts create our reality, therefore our thoughts create our stressful reality. The power of Pause Breathe Proceed begins in the pause to become self-aware and situationally aware of our stressors. What is causing our alert systems to flash?

Stress is a catch-all term used to put all the challenging emotions into one bottle. Dig deeper to figure out what is causing the stress. Anger? Resentment? Expectations? When we become aware of our current thoughts, emotions and feelings and look at them from all angles, we can understand what is going on within us. Stress comes in many forms. What stresses one person may seem like nothing to another.

What is truly causing your "stress?" Know yourself. Use your Pause Breathe Proceed credo card and daily routine, and own your responses. What emotions and feelings are you experiencing that challenge you? Make choices not excuses.

Say the emotion out loud as if you were looking it in the eyes. Name it to tame it. Take away the power of the emotion by putting it on notice, "I see you and you will not destroy my day."

The killer of stress is what is known as the fight, flight, or freeze mode. Stress releases adrenaline and cortisol into our bodies so we can react quickly to danger. This mode was meant for true survival such as running from a bear or any danger that requires a strong, quick reaction. The stress mode is not meant for daily living, like it has become. Continuous rushes of adrenaline and cortisol exhaust the body.

Pause Breathe Proceed brings awareness to the a situation and reminds us to pause and breathe. Are you really in a dangerous situation? Deep belly breathing will alert the Vegas nerve to tell the brain to switch to the parasympathetic mode (rest and digest) from the sympathetic mode (fight, flight, or freeze). We have the power to change the chemical responses in our body. How cool is that?

Pause to become aware of your thoughts. A calm thought can trump a stressful thought. A response can beat a reaction. Peace can reign over anger. Every situation can have a pause-itive outcome. A pause-itive outcome doesn't mean every situation is full of rainbows and unicorns. It could mean that you finally understand why you react the way you do. No one said life wouldn't be hard. If a belly breath isn't creating calm, perhaps walk away. Go somewhere and scream, cry, or laugh. Head into nature. Jump up and down. Dance like no one is watching. Just get the energy out of you.

What or who stresses you? What thoughts about the situation or the person are causing you distress? What emotions come up? Dig in. Is it an opinion? A belief? Can you change your thoughts or your perspective? What else is true about this situation or person that is pause-itive?

"Between *stimulus* and *response* there is a space.
In that space is our power to choose our response.
In our response lies our growth and freedom."

– Victor Frankyl

Pause

Superpowers: self-awareness and situational awareness

The pause is the "WHAT am I about to say, do, or what am I thinking?" Pausing before reacting and becoming aware of what is happening around and within you requires the ability to break a subconscious habit. Without pause, reactions are triggered.

It can be challenging to change habits that have been a part of your life for so long. Deciding whether a habit is still relevant and changing those that are not is critical to personal growth. This takes time, but don't get discouraged. Start now. Once you change habits, you change from within and it is freedom.

"Conscious" is what you are aware of. "Subconscious" is that which you are not fully aware; however, it influences your actions and feelings.

Subconscious habits are the brain's way of firing neurons that direct the body and mind to react to certain stimuli, situations or people. The subconscious triggers the mind and body to react the same way it has in the past. Neurons that wire together fire together; they know what to do when that situation arises again. The more they fire together, the more you repeat an action, the more strongly the habit is formed. It's like having an instruction book that your mind constantly refers to. Everyone's instruction book is different as it was written by the people in your life: parents, siblings, friends, teachers, pastors, and others.

In *Becoming Supernatural*, Dr. Joe Dispenza, explains that as thoughts arise, they create a feeling via a chemical reaction in our body. That chemical reaction triggers our emotions. That whole process – thought, feeling, and emotion – create a memory. When that memory arises again, the associated emotions and chemical reactions follow. This emotional energy creates an attachment and often an addiction to that chemical response in our body. An addiction to that old thought. According to Dr. Dispenza, a memory without an emotional charge is called wisdom.

This makes sense to me. For example, my ex-husband used to give me yellow roses for special occasions. After the divorce, every time I saw a yellow rose I would think of him. I would get emotional and my feelings (chemical reaction) would turn my stomach upside down. That memory would ruin my day.

I decided to practice Pause Breathe Proceed with yellow roses. I paused with self-awareness and situational awareness. I let the memories surface. I became aware of all the emotions and feelings that the yellow rose created. I took deep belly breaths with understanding and compassion for myself, my ex, and our situation. I processed my emotions and feelings. I sat with them, understood them, and gave myself grace for what I had been through.

My past does not and will not define my future. I kept breathing until I felt calm.

I proceeded with forgiveness and kindness. I replaced the feelings and

emotions of sadness, disappointment and anger with the beauty of the rose and the joy I felt moving forward.

The key is moving forward. It is hard to remove the emotional charge of a memory or thought if you allow yourself to get stuck in that time and place. We are not meant to be stagnant. Life is to be lived, explored, and to thrive. Turn challenging emotional energy into wisdom. Know that you are strong and can move on to bigger and better things.

Science has proven that the brain can rewire neurons. It has neuroplasticity. We can change the way we react to a situation by pausing which stops that neural pattern from firing. We can then change the way we respond which will rewire the neurons to fire in a new pattern. The more the new response is practiced, the easier it gets. Practice is key to retrain the brain.

Try to change a habit: the way you get ready for the day, the hand you use to eat, your daily routine, the order of your apps on your phone, the route you take to work or school. Is it challenging? What new things do you notice? Put some Pause Breathe Proceed reminders up and try again. Does it get easier as you practice?

What are some habits you want to change? Use your Pause Breathe Proceed stickers, bracelet, daily routine, and other reminders to catch that habit before you do it, then redirect. What new habits are you forming?

Write down your experience when you pause. What thoughts, reactions, feelings, or emotions arise? What is going on inside of you? What is going on around you?

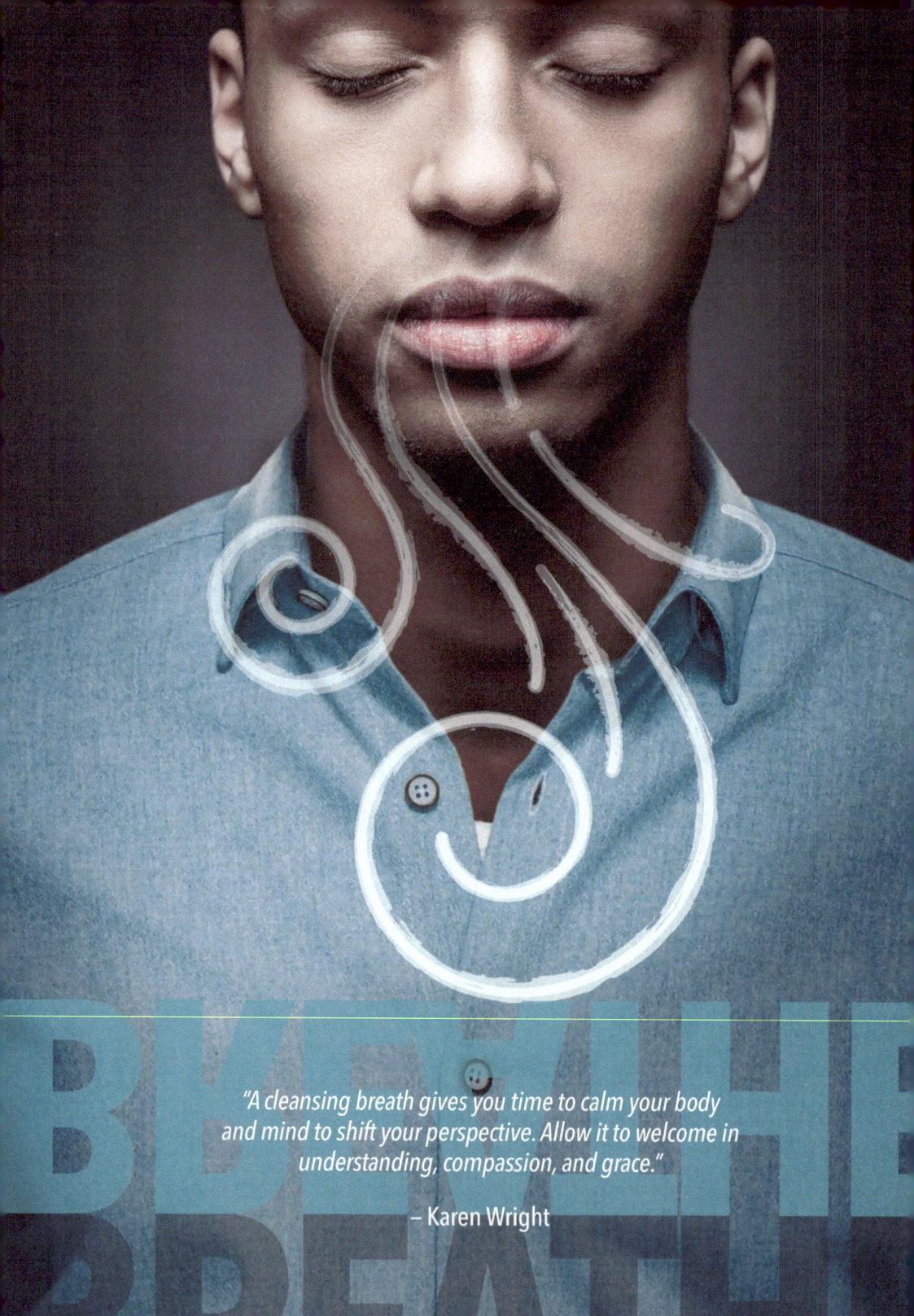

Breathe

Superpowers: understanding and compassion

The breath gives us life and so much more. A deep breath gives us time to understand our reactions and ask ourselves "why?" Reactions reflect what we are thinking and how we are feeling. Check in. Take responsibility. Don't take problems out on someone else. The breath calms your body and mind. It gives you control over your response. Without the breath, every trigger can lead to a reaction. Words spoken cannot be taken back. Pause and breathe.

Understanding creates a perspective shift from "me" to "we." Compassion is about being in the present moment without judgment or anger. Be curious. Maybe the other person just got bad news or is having a bad day. Be compassionate. Maybe you aren't feeling well. Understand where you are at. What is really going on? Being right is relative and subject to opinion. Being understanding and compassionate is so much more rewarding.

One morning I was cranky toward my husband. He finally said, "Pause and breathe." I became aware that my hands were sore, my body was tired, and I had a full day of massage clients. I had taken my feeling of anxiety out on him. Self-awareness and situational awareness, the pause, followed by a deep belly breath, understanding and compassion would have prevented this misunderstanding and my need to apologize.

Once I understood the situation, I had compassion for myself and my husband. Had I started my day with my Pause Breathe Proceed routine of checking in, I would have realized that I was going to be more reactive that day because I was in pain.

We take up to 23,000 breaths per day. Breath is often taken for granted until it is jeopardized. As an athlete, massage therapist, and recovering stress addict I appreciate a good belly breath. Belly breathing encourages full oxygen exchange, slows the heartbeat, and triggers the Vagus nerve. The Vagus nerve is the gut-brain communicator. When you belly breathe, the Vagus nerve signals the brain to calm the body and mind down. It's the CHILL OUT code.

Put one hand on your chest and one hand on your belly and breathe. Notice where your breath is coming from. Does your chest or belly expand? Chest breathing is stress breathing. Create belly breathing habits to stay calm.

According to Mayo Clinic, "During stressful moments, conscious breathing allows you to shift and release negative energy instead of storing it in your body. This is important, because stored-up energy often manifests as muscle tension and other physical ailments. Although breathing is something your body naturally does, it's also a skill that can be sharpened."

Box breathing is an easy-to-use breathing style that can be incorporated into your day at any time. Imagine a square. Inhale for 4 seconds, hold for 4 seconds, exhale for 4+ seconds, hold for 4 seconds, repeat. Focus on your belly expanding. The pause for 4 counts during breathing brings you to the present moment because the body and mind say, "Hey we need air, what is going on?"

I like the fact that I own my body and mind. My mind can say, "Now that I have your attention, let's calm down."

Notice the deep belly breaths you take throughout the day. After you pause, inhale and exhale. Did you find understanding and compassion for a challenge you are facing? Do you feel your shoulders drop down and relax? Did you find a moment of peace and calm? Did your perspective shift?

Belly breathe/box breathe. Inhale, pause, exhale, pause. Scan your mind: what thoughts are popping up? Scan your body; what emotions and feelings arise? Where in your body do you feel tightness or stress? Why? Keep asking why and get to the real reason. Own your body and mind. Let the breath calm and relax you, releasing understanding and compassion. Write down your breathwork experience. The more you practice, the more powerful your breath will vitalize your mind and body.

PROCEED

"I've learned that people will forget what you said, people will forget what you did, but people will never forget how you made them feel."

– Maya Angelou

Proceed

Superpowers: kindness and forgiveness

How we proceed directly affects who we are, reveals the values we hold true, and determines our true character. Everyone is struggling with something. Knowing why isn't imperative. Be kind and forgive.

Holding grudges or anger only hurts you. Not forgiving yourself is holding a grudge against yourself and doesn't make sense. It is negative energy from a past situation. Choose to process it, let it go and move forward. Keep the present and the future clear of all negativity.

We have made choices that may not have been the right choices but we did the best we could at the time. Give yourself and those around you grace. No one is perfect. Choose to find pause-itivity with kindness and forgiveness. When you forgive, you heal your inner world. When you show kindness, you heal your outer world.

Proceeding in kindness and forgiveness will shift the energy within you, around you, and ultimately the energy of this world. In a world that needs more kindness and forgiveness, be generous with both.

A friend got in my face in anger. I paused and breathed. When she was done, I simply walked out of the room. I needed space to calm my body and mind with my breath. Prior to Pause Breathe Proceed this hot-tempered redhead would have unleashed on her. I now know that silence is a powerful tool. After a few weeks, we talked about our disagreement in a respectful manner. I later realized it took courage to speak to me instead of running to others. Although I didn't agree with her tone and everything she said, I heard her. I thanked her for coming to me with her concerns.

Addressing a situation or person may take days, weeks or months. It may result in a discussion and finding understanding and forgiveness. One way or another, get rid of the pent-up energy and learn the lesson that was presented to you.

Kindness and forgiveness start within. Is there something you need to forgive yourself or someone else for? Write down your plan of action to find forgiveness. Breathe and keep breathing until you can forgive. Forgiveness removes their power over you.

What can you do today to be kind to yourself? What can you do to be kind to someone else? Create this habit and watch your day become magical.

Reaction vs. response

A reaction comes from a stressed state of mind. A response comes from a peaceful state of mind. Find peace of mind before you give a piece of your mind.

A reaction is often done in an instant without much thought. It is our subconscious, our habitual response system taking action without regard to consequences. A response is a thoughtful reply, using both instincts and the conscious mind, and considers the consequences. Reacting is emotional whereas responding is emotional intelligence.

How do you train yourself to respond versus react? Practice the pause every time you feel your emotions rising, the hair on the back of your neck standing up, the need to lash out, or you've lost your peace of mind. Pause. Breathe. Do not proceed. A reaction typically leads to hurt feelings and apologies. Become aware of your thoughts, feelings, and emotions so you can control how you respond. Spread love not hate.

It's interesting when you learn to pause and breathe and remain silent versus reacting. Silence is powerful. It shows you are in control of your emotions and evaluating the situation. You will earn respect as you reply with a well-thought response.

Practice the daily Pause Breathe Proceed routine two to three times a day. Be aware of how you are feeling physically, mentally, and emotionally from morning to evening. Belly breathe as emotions and feelings arise. Be curious about what is going on. Understand how your thoughts, emotions and feelings directly affect your interactions with the outside world.

Pause Breathe Proceed will become natural as you incorporate it in your daily life. Once you know it, you can't unknow it. Pause Breathe Proceed will bring less reactivity, stress, anger, frustration and more understanding, compassion, kindness, and forgiveness. It is a practice, so use it daily and often.

Record your reactions and your responses throughout the day. The more you catch yourself reacting, the more you will understand yourself and the easier it will be to respond before reacting. Who do you owe an apology due to a reaction? Who was reactive to you and owes you an apology? How will you feel if you never get an apology? Can you find compassion, forgiveness and grace for that person?

"There is nothing in this world
that can trouble you
as much as your own thoughts."

– Unknown

Origin of our thoughts

Know your thoughts and you will be the master of your universe. You have the power to keep a thought or change it. Either choice will create the life you live.

Pause and be curiously aware of thoughts, feelings and emotions as they rise to the surface. Emotions animate our life. They will come and go so befriend them. Hello sadness, I know you had to visit me. Please hold my hand as I walk through this sad time. I know joy, laughter, anxiety, and many more will visit me for they animate my days.

We are frequently told what to think, say, and do. We have been influenced by parents, grandparents, friends, teachers, pastors, employers, social media, and the list goes on. Each influencer has written their opinions in our book of life. We have many authors and many chapters in our book. We took their words at face value and plugged them into our subconscious. They were written in our book. Those opinions that we held as truth and believe in will affect us for the rest of our life. Pause.

Breathe: who are the authors of your thoughts?

As thoughts arise, take a deep breath and ask where they came from? Do they resonate within? Thoughts may be from a different generation. Check in whether a thought is true to this day. Does it feel right? Can you visualize a different way?

Proceed is your chance to pivot and change your thoughts. You can become the author of the next chapters in your life. You can shift the narrative if it doesn't align with your values and goals or no longer applies to your generation. If it doesn't feel right, discover a new thought. Look at the situation from all angles and change the story you tell yourself. What else is true about that thought?

This is your chance to create the life that resides in your dreams. This is the chance to say, "I choose to move forward in life my way. I make choices that align with my goals, values, dreams, and visions."

The self-awareness and situational awareness of the pause, combined with the understanding and compassion of the breath, empowers a decision of how best to move forward in this time and space to proceed in kindness and forgiveness.

Notice your thoughts as they arise, and become curious. Who told you it was true? If you don't know that is OK, do they feel right? How can they change? Finding your truth requires you to challenge your thoughts and feelings. Who are you? Who do people think you are? Who do you want to be? Are your thoughts kind and considerate or angry and resentful? Knowing your thoughts gives you a powerful insight into who you are. You then have the information you need to pivot.

Reminders

**Without a reminder to pause,
practice, and become self-aware,
you continue to live self-unaware.**

Reminders are needed to pause and check in with the body and mind. Without a reminder, it is nearly impossible to override the neurons trained to fire and repeat that which it knows. In the absence of awareness of your thoughts, they are open for manipulation. Thoughts that are anchored in values, goals, and dreams are less likely to be swayed by others. Social media, the government, your friends, and others want you to think their way. Use reminders to remember to check in with your thoughts anchored in your values so you can proudly proceed.

Write down ways you can remember to pause and breathe throughout the day. Set a schedule and use your credo card, bracelet, stickers, and alarms to remind yourself to pause and breathe before you proceed.

"If you are positive, you'll see opportunities instead of obstacles."

– Confucius

Pause-itivity

In every situation you have the choice to be positive or negative. Being positive will change you from the inside out and create a wave of positivity that will ripple through the situation.

Pause-itivity is the art of pausing when faced with a negative in order to become positive or optimistic in attitude. In every situation, we have a choice to be positive or negative. I believe there is no good or bad, there just is. How you look at a situation or person is influenced by how you feel and what you're thinking at that moment.

Own your response. Understand what is truly going on. Your first impression, gut instinct, is powerful. Never discount what your soul is telling you.

After your first impression, pause and take in your self-awareness and situational awareness. What influences are you bringing to the situation? What is happening around you? How do you feel and why? Take a moment or a few days, however long you need, to understand the situation and why your perception of the situation is what it is. What other factors are influencing you? What else is true?

I am not suggesting that you ignore feelings that are "negative." They are real for you. Sit with them. Process them. If you hold them in, they can resurface at any moment. Look your feelings straight in the eyes and understand why they are coming up. How can you pivot?

Write down the negative influences in your life. What makes them negative? Can you shift your perspective and find a pause-itive? What else is true about the situation that can shed light on it and make it positive? Is it time to remove yourself from toxic people and situations in your life? It is YOUR life after all.

"Remember that stress doesn't come from what's going on in your life.
It comes from your thoughts about what's going on in your life."

– Andrew Bernstein

Stress awareness

Become self-aware of your stress levels throughout the day so you can own the thoughts that are creating the reality you are living. Pause. Breathe. Proceed.

Without being self-aware, how can we understand what is causing our stress? If we dig deep we can find the emotional thought-provoking culprits causing our stress levels to rise. Without emotional intelligence the body and mind keep going and going until we "stress out."

What if we regularly acknowledge our stress level and take time to decompress? As we pause throughout the day we can identify what is causing our stress. Using our breath we can then calm our mind (thoughts) and body (feelings and emotions). By addressing the state of our body and mind throughout the day, we can proceed appropriately.

Taking this mindful moment to know ourselves gives us the emotional intelligence to decompress, unwind, take a moment, shift the narrative of our stressful thoughts, own them, process them, and let them go. There is space to find a way to bring peace into the mind and body.

Refer to your credo card often throughout the day, perhaps set specific times to perform the calm routine.

Daily routine

Pause Breathe Proceed is a practice. Once you know it, you can't unknow it. It will change your life from the inside out. Create a Pause Breathe Proceed routine and watch the magic unfold.

They say practice makes perfect, so practice what you want in your life. Pause Breathe Proceed is the practice of getting to know ourselves. It is as powerful as physical exercise.

When we stop doing something, we fall back into the same old habits. To get physically strong, we may practice biking, running, walking, hiking, kayaking, paddle boarding, softball, baseball or climbing.

To get mentally strong, we must be aware and take ownership of our thoughts, feelings, and emotions. We must practice knowing ourselves. What is going on inside? Knowing this, we can decide how to move forward. We can know how to be still and decompress, or how to walk away and reset.

Use the Pause Breathe Proceed daily routine to find calm, check in, and move through your day with peace. Use the bracelets and stickers as reminders to pause and breathe. Share the practice with others so they will reduce their stress and you can work together for accountability.

1. **Pause** – self-awareness and situational awareness

2. **Breathe** – understanding and compassion, without judgment.

3. **Proceed** – forgiveness and kindness toward yourself and others.

Carry your credo card with you. This will help you remember why and how to pause breathe proceed.

Chaos is the absence of a plan

How many thoughts a day go towards your goals and dreams?

Without a plan, life just keeps moving, directed by the events happening in our life. We accomplish very little. When I had down time, I'd jump on social media to see what was up. I now realize I spent too much time looking at what everyone else was doing and not enough time on what I wanted out of life. I got comfortable just existing, which can be OK for a time but may also lead to regrets. Excuses replace hopes and dreams. Dreams? Goals? I forgot I had any. Time starts flying by and dreams get buried. One day you wonder what happened.

Without a plan, or even a sketch, life goes sideways, up, down, and you barely move forward. With a plan, you have a compass, a direction to move forward, the hope that each choice you now consciously make will move you closer to your dreams.

Notice who and what grabs your attention throughout the day. Pay attention, like we are constantly told as kids. Big media is making money off grabbing your attention and sucking you into ads. Take your attention back and put it toward building the rest of your life.

Welcome to the Pause Breathe Proceed journey! Enjoy, be curious, and get to know yourself.

"Slow down and enjoy life. It's not only the scenery you miss by going too fast, you also miss the sense of where you are going and why."

– Eddie Cantor

Slow down

**Slowing down will naturally
calm your central nervous system.**

Why are we in such a hurry to go nowhere? We rush and rush, our sympathetic nervous system (fight, flight, or freeze) stays on high alert, and our body fatigues. This can bring depression, anxiety, and disappointment. We fill our days with things that "have to get done," but do they? We create the life we live. What excuses are you making that is causing the fast-paced chaos in your days?

Slow down! Pause! Breathe! When the body walks, talks, and eats more slowly the parasympathetic nervous system (rest and digest) takes over and we feel a sense of calm. Moving slower puts you in the conductor's seat of the freight train of your life. Slow it down or get crazy and pull the emergency brake lever and stop. Just be. Observe. Breathe. Listen. Learn. This is your life. Understand it so you can create the life you dream of. You got this! It may not be easy but anything worth having rarely is. I believe in YOU!

Do no harm

"Virtue lies in our power, and similarly so does vice; because where it is in our power to act, it is also in our power not to act."

– Aristotle

Throughout this document, thoughts, emotions, and feelings have been discussed. As you explore all three, be curious about them and you will learn about yourself. They are intertwined to give us our body, mind, and soul connection. As you examine them you may discover who planted a seed in your head for a thought. If you disagree it doesn't make that person wrong, they just have a different perspective based on what they know, how they were raised, and what they believe. As mentioned above, we are all raised differently therefore we all have a different perspective on life which drives our thoughts.

As you can see there are many layers and many tentacles to our thoughts, feelings, and emotions. They are energetic entities that reside within our mind and body. Once you put a thought, feeling, or emotion into action, it creates a change. It becomes energy in motion and can create a positive or negative impact on yourself or someone else.

Virtue is moral excellence. A virtue is a trait or quality that is deemed to be morally good and thus is valued as a foundation of principle and good moral being. In other words, it is a behavior that shows high moral standards. Live by high moral standards; patience, kindness, honesty, respect, courage, responsibility, and all virtues that bring light and hope into this world.

As you pause and breathe to examine your thoughts, feelings, and emotions let virtues guide your decision on how you will proceed.

Pause, and everything will change!